W9-CKI-364

DATE DUE			

**BIO
JAMES**

33577000663748
Rappoport, Ken.

Lebron James : king
on and off the court

SPORTS STARS WITH HEART

LeBron James

KING ON AND OFF THE COURT

by Ken Rappoport

Enslow Publishers, Inc.

40 Industrial Road
Box 398
Berkeley Heights, NJ 07922
USA
http://www.enslow.com

Library of Congress Cataloging-in-Publication Data

Rappoport, Ken.
  Lebron James : king on and off the court / Ken Rappoport. — 1st ed.
      p. cm. — (Sports stars with heart)
  Includes bibliographical references and index.
  ISBN-10: 0-7660-2420-2
  1. James, LeBron—Juvenile literature. 2. Basketball players—United
States—Biography—Juvenile literature. I. Title. II. Series.
  GV884.J36R37 2006
  796.323092—dc22
  [B]   2006012538

Credits

Editorial Direction: Red Line Editorial, Inc. (Bob Temple)
Editor: Sue Green
Designer: Lindaanne Donohoe
Revision Editor: Jeff Stahlhut

ISBN-13: 978-0-7660-2420-5

Printed in the United States of America

10 9 8 7 6 5 4 3

Photographs © 2006: AP Photo/Ed Bailey: 80; AP Photo/Ed Betz: 59; AP Photo/Chris Carlson: 45; AP Photo/Tony Dejak: 8, 33; AP Photo/Mark Duncan: 3, 39, 47, 93, 97, 111; AP Photo/Tina Fineberg: 85; AP Photo/Scott R. Galvin: 35; AP Photo/Jay LaPrete: 53; AP Photo/Nike, Phil Long: 109; AP Photo/Akron Beacon Journal, Phil Masturzo: 17; AP Photo/Mike Mergen: 60; AP Photo/Rich Pedroncelli: 4; AP Photo/J.D. Pooley: 18, 25; AP Photo/Jeff Roberson: 68; AP Photo/Rich Schultz: 50; AP Photo/Ron Schwane: 3, 29, 54, 72, 77, 79, 105; AP Photo/Mark Terrill: 1, 3; AP Photo/George Widman: 64; AP Photo/Steve Yeater: 12

Cover Photo: The Cleveland Cavaliers' LeBron James dunks during the NBA Rookie Challenge February 18, 2005, at the Pepsi Center in Denver.

CONTENTS

James goes up for a layup in a game against the Sacramento Kings.

CHAPTER ONE

Opening Night

It was a dream come true, but it could quickly turn into a nightmare.

Ever since he was a youngster, LeBron James dreamed of playing in the National Basketball Association (NBA). And now, on October 29, 2003, he was playing in his first official NBA game with the Cleveland Cavaliers. Their opponents were the Sacramento Kings, one of the NBA's stronger teams.

The Akron, Ohio, native was the most publicized player ever to make the jump from high school to the NBA. He was also the richest. James had signed a $90 million sneaker deal with Nike, along with other lucrative offers. Even before he took his first NBA shot, he was making more endorsement money than anyone in the league.

But was James good enough to live up to the

MICHAEL JORDAN'S NBA DEBUT

LeBron James considers Michael Jordan his inspiration and basketball hero, and many consider Jordan the greatest to ever play the game. So how does James' NBA debut compare with Jordan's? Against the Washington Bullets on October 26, 1984, Jordan played 40 minutes, scored a total of 16 points, and had 7 assists. James, against the Sacramento Kings, played 42 minutes, scored 25 points, and added 9 assists.

tremendous hype? Or would his dream take a bad turn and become a nightmare?

James was only eighteen years old. He would be playing against hardened professionals. There would be no mercy shown to basketball's newest phenomenon, who was regarded by many as the "next Michael Jordan."

James had added to his growing legend by wearing the same number 23 on his uniform as Jordan, his inspiration and basketball hero.

The media hordes that had followed James all through training camp and the exhibition season seemed to be growing with each day. And now they had descended on ARCO Arena in Sacramento to witness the most hyped debut in NBA history since Larry Bird and Magic Johnson entered the league in 1979.

The Kings had issued 350 media credentials, twice the number for a normal regular-season game. There was a playoff atmosphere in the arena.

Ever since the previous spring when James had been the number one pick in the NBA Draft by the Cavaliers, the star-conscious league had been building toward this game. There were days of commercials featuring James leading up to the opener. The NBA, hoping to find a superstar to fill the void left by the retired Jordan, had billed the contest on its Web site as "King James vs. the Kings."

"King James" was the nickname mostly used to describe the super-talented basketball prodigy. But he was also known as "Elvis" to some. Bob Donewald, the Cavaliers' assistant coach assigned to help James through his rookie season, had nicknamed the player after legendary singer Elvis Presley.

"Why Elvis?" Donewald said. "Just look at the entourage that follows LeBron wherever he goes: the media, the fans. If Elvis came back to life, I couldn't imagine it being any more of a circus."[1]

So now "Elvis" was in the house, and the arena was buzzing with anticipation.

LIVING UP TO THE HYPE

Along with a sellout crowd at ARCO, millions more would be watching on national television. ESPN was following James' every movement down to the last detail—even a closeup of James clipping his toenails in the locker room!

James' popularity was evident in the marketing of his replica jerseys. Nearly half a million had been sold before he had played his first game.

James had promised the media he would "go out on this court and showcase some of my talent, my teammates' talents and showcase that we're supposed to be here."[2]

James was regarded in Cleveland as the savior of a troubled franchise. The year before, the Cavaliers had a miserable 17–65 record and finished as a lottery-pick team.

James works on his shot during practice at Gund Arena in Cleveland.

But things brightened considerably when they won the lottery and made James their first pick.

DID YOU KNOW?

With the chance to draft a player who had grown up in Akron, all of Ohio went wild when the Cavaliers drew the first pick of the 2003 NBA Draft lottery. LeBron James, it seemed, would be playing in his home state. But was James' selection really a slam-dunk for the Cavs? Probably so, but did you know how many other stars were taken in the first round of that draft? Carmelo Anthony, Chris Bosh, Dwyane Wade, Kirk Hinrich, and Luke Ridnour are just a few of the big-name players drafted after James.

Before the game against the Kings, James had been asked by reporters if anyone had called to wish him luck.

"All of Ohio," he said.[3]

James had struggled early in the preseason, averaging just 8 points a game and making merely 33 percent of his shots in the first three exhibition games.

Cavaliers coach Paul Silas acknowledged James' slow start.

"His first few exhibition games weren't stellar by any means," Silas said. "I wondered if he was going to accept that. But in practice he worked even harder."[4]

By the fifth game of the exhibition season, Silas

LEBRON FILE

Height: 6' 8"

Weight: 240 pounds

Date of birth: Dec. 30, 1984

Position: Forward

High school: St. Vincent-St. Mary High School

NBA team: Cleveland Cavaliers

Acquired: First-round (first overall) draft pick, 2003

Hometown: Akron, Ohio

had handed James the highly responsible point guard position. His job was to bring the ball up the court and get plays started.

James couldn't be classified for one position, however. At six feet eight inches and 240 pounds, he could easily be placed at forward. He could even serve as a shooting guard when the occasion demanded.

"He just has that swagger about him that says, 'You know, I'm pretty good at this thing,'" Silas said.[5]

With all the attention he was getting, James was bound to have some opening-night jitters. He did—but it didn't affect his game against the Kings.

Even the first quarter was full of highlights for James.

He won a rebound battle with Doug Christie and dumped the Kings' forward to the floor. James dribbled the length of the court and passed to Ricky Davis for a dunk.

He connected on a baseline jump shot over Mike Bibby. He launched a 16-footer over seven-footer Brad Miller for 2 points. On a fast break, he brought the crowd to its feet when he looked right and hit Davis with a bounce pass to his left. Davis put in an easy layup.

James looked spectacular, scoring 12 points in the first quarter alone. But it was an unspectacular play that perhaps defined his game the most.

James got the ball on a breakaway and easily could have driven down court for an uncontested shot. Instead, he passed the ball to Davis for a dunk.

"I'm a team player," he said later. "He's the scorer, I'm a point guard."[6]

It was one of 9 assists that night for James. He also scored 25 points on 12-of-20 shooting, grabbed 6 rebounds, and made 4 steals in a great all-around game that reminded observers of the great Magic Johnson.

LeBron James had done everything for his team, more than most expected, considering all the pressure. The only thing he couldn't do was deliver a

LEBRON'S FIRST NBA GAME

Opponent: Sacramento Kings

Off to a great start: 12 first-quarter points

Grand totals: 25 points, 6 rebounds, 4 steals, and 9 assists in 42 minutes played

James passes the ball as he flies through the air.

victory for the Cavs, who lost 106–92.

He was on the floor for 42 minutes in a dazzling debut by comparison with other high school hotshots who had jumped to the pros. Kobe Bryant and Tracy McGrady, to name two, had each played only 6 minutes in their first NBA starts and scored no points. And Kevin Garnett played 16 minutes and scored 8 points.

None of them had assumed natural leadership of an NBA team so early in their careers. So the future seemed limitless for the NBA's newest star.

"Running up and down with

MOST POINTS BY A ROOKIE IN AN NBA GAME
Wilt Chamberlain scored 58 points on January 25, 1960, for Philadelphia against Detroit. On February 21, 1960, he again dropped in 58 against New York. James, by comparison, scored a rookie-season high 41 on March 27, 2004, against New Jersey.

the NBA players, it's a dream," James said. "I was just fortunate to get some shots, and they fell through."[7]

He said he didn't change much from his high school style.

"I was able to make a lot of moves I used in high school," James said. "I just had to bring a lot more power. They're a lot stronger in the NBA."[8]

He was only doing what came naturally. For as long as anyone could remember, James had always been a dominant force in basketball.

Although LeBron James had made basketball look easy, he had not been granted an easy road to follow early in his life.

CHAPTER TWO

Growing Up in Akron

LeBron James was scared. He ducked for cover when he heard the shots. He did not want to end up like some of his neighbors, lying facedown in a pool of blood in an alley or sitting in a jail cell.

This wasn't some make-believe action movie scene made in Hollywood. It was part of his life while growing up in dangerous neighborhoods in Akron, Ohio.

"I saw drugs, guns, killings," LeBron said. "It was crazy."[1]

Born to Gloria James on December 30, 1984, LeBron first lived with his mother and grandmother, Freda, in a comfortable home. But when LeBron's grandmother died suddenly, they were forced to live a

FACTS ON AKRON, OHIO

- Ten million people live within a 241-kilometer (150-mile) radius of Akron.
- Fifty percent of the American population lives within a 805-kilometer (500-mile) radius of Akron.
- Akron is the fifth largest city in Ohio.
- Akron is the home of the Akron Aeros, the Cleveland Indians' AA Minor League baseball team.
- Once known as the "Rubber Capital of the World," Akron is now a world-renowned center for polymer research and development. There are 400 polymer-related companies located in the Akron area.
- In 1994, Akron ranked ninth in the nation by *Site Selection* magazine for locating new manufacturing plants.
- In June 2005, Akron was ranked 16th by Farmers Insurance Group of Companies as the Most Secure Place to Live (Large Metro Area).
- The name "Akron" was derived from a Greek word meaning "high."
- Akron was founded in 1825.

nomadic life—drifting from place to place, mostly staying with friends. There was usually not enough money to pay the rent for an apartment of their own.

When LeBron and his mother did find their own place, they did not stay long. One of the buildings they lived in was condemned and destroyed by the

DID YOU KNOW?

LeBron James was born on December 30, 1984. He shares that birthday with golfer Tiger Woods, who was born on December 30, 1975.

Others born on December 30:

• Sandy Koufax (1935), pitcher for the Brooklyn and Los Angeles Dodgers

• A.J. Pierzynski (1976), catcher for the Chicago White Sox

• Kenyon Martin (1977), plays for NBA's Denver Nuggets

• Bo Diddley (1928), singer, songwriter

• Michael Nesmith (1942), singer, songwriter, member of the Monkees

• Davy Jones (1945), singer, also a member of the Monkees

• Matt Lauer (1957), NBC *Today* host

• Tracey Ullman (1959), English singer, actress

city. When LeBron was five years old, he and his mother were forced to move seven times.

When he was in fourth grade, LeBron's unsettled life caused trouble in school. That year, he missed 82 days of classes.

James follows along as his mother Gloria, reads to children in Akron.

James celebrates an Irish win with his mother.

But LeBron remembered his mother did her best to protect him, provide love, and surround him with caring people.

"My mom kept food in my mouth and clothes on my back," LeBron said.[2]

If not for Gloria James and a group of caring friends, it's likely LeBron would be anywhere else but on the bright stage of the NBA today.

"My mother is my everything," LeBron says. "Always has been. Always will be."[3]

LeBron never knew his father. He found someone else to take his place—Eddie Jackson. As Gloria James' boyfriend, he became an important part of LeBron's life.

Jackson and LeBron hit it off right away. As a youngster, LeBron loved wrestling and other rough games. He liked to jump off the couch and land on top of Jackson, often with a resounding thud!

Jackson didn't mind serving as a human landing cushion for the little boy. But before long, he found something a little safer for LeBron to do. He bought him a basketball set, complete with basketball, hoop, backboard, and stand. When Jackson set it up for him, LeBron was thrilled. Suddenly, the young boy was hooked on the sport.

INSTANT STAR

LeBron remembers he was nine years old when he first played organized basketball. "I played for a team called the Summer Lake Hornets," LeBron said. "I was playing before that, just around the 'hood, but that was my first organized team."[4]

LeBron was an instant star. "I was good. I worked at it a little bit, but in all honesty, the game came naturally to me."[5]

When he first started playing basketball, LeBron was tall and skilled, according to one coach, but not much different from most boys his age.

"He really liked to shoot the ball—a lot," said Dru Joyce II, who coached LeBron in grade school and then high school. "I started telling LeBron about passing the ball, how great players make their teammates better. I talked about getting his shots in the flow of the game."[6]

That was the last time Joyce ever had to tell LeBron about shooting too much.

THE JAMES FAMILY FOUNDATION

The James Family Foundation, established in April 2005, is about hope, help, and heart. The mission of the foundation is to build hope in the lives of children and families in the community who are dealing with adversity. Without hope, there is no will to improve one's circumstances in life. Helping children and families, particularly those headed by single mothers, achieve more through education, recreation, employment, and better health are ways the foundation seeks to work in the local community and worldwide. The foundation has a heart for people regardless of age, race, family, or economic status. It is committed to helping those who have the heart and dedication to succeed. For more information, visit www.lebronfoundation.org.

"He just got it. He started passing the ball. You only have to tell him things once," Joyce said.[7]

CHANGE OF SCENERY

Frankie Walker, LeBron's youth basketball coach, knew the boy had been struggling in school and his life needed more stability. Walker invited LeBron to live with his family for a while, just until LeBron could get himself straightened out. Gloria James accepted the offer. She felt LeBron's life could only get better living with the Walkers.

Walker had always found LeBron to be a very coachable basketball player and a quick learner. He had a built-in sense for the game. He always listened and worked hard on the court. Now he would be part of a disciplined family life that stressed hard work and responsibility in other areas of his life.

"It changed my life," LeBron said. "The next year I had perfect attendance and a B average."[8]

LeBron actually started enjoying school. His favorite subject was earth science. He learned about the earth and how planets such as Jupiter and Mars related to his world.

"I love exploring," he said. "I always found that stuff really interesting."[9]

GLORIA JAMES ON LEBRON

As told to Tim Rogers of the *Cleveland Plain Dealer*:

"People ask me all the time when I knew LeBron was going to become a star," said Gloria James. "I tell them that he was born a star. I am very proud of him, and not just because of the basketball. In 17 years, I've never had to whip him or punish him. Throughout school, from elementary to middle to St. Vincent-St. Mary, he has maintained good grades. It seems he's always been on the merit roll and even made the honor roll."

By sixth grade, LeBron was dividing his time between Walker's home and his mother's. Gloria James was working, and Eddie Jackson was providing additional financial support with his jobs as a drug counselor and concert promoter.

Meanwhile, basketball was becoming a big part of LeBron's life. He was hotly competitive and hated to lose.

GIVING BACK TO HIS HOMETOWN

Through his nonprofit James Family Foundation, James announced in August 2005 that 1,000 backpacks full of school supplies would be distributed to youngsters in Akron and Cleveland. Through his foundation and Target, James personally distributed the supplies.

Dru Joyce II coached LeBron on a summer league team before later coaching him in high school. He remembers LeBron coming over to his house to play basketball against his son, Dru Joyce III.

"Our guys didn't play a lot of street ball where they'd pick up bad habits," Joyce II said. "They played a lot against each other. LeBron and my son used to play one-on-one in my driveway.

"They were so competitive, I had them stop after the sixth grade. They were best friends, but they kept wanting to fight each other after those games."[10]

LeBron's startling basketball talents were starting

to be noticed. While playing in eighth grade in a students-versus-teachers game, he soared into the air for his first dunk shot. He was fourteen.

By this time, LeBron was already a rising basketball star in the community. He gained attention when he led his eighth-grade team to the finals of a tournament sponsored by the Amateur Athletic Union (AAU).

Although he was primarily known as a basketball player, LeBron also starred in football. He would be a good catch for any of the athletic programs in the area high schools.

LeBron had his choice of any of them. He decided to accept a scholarship to go to St. Vincent-St. Mary, a small private school with a solid basketball reputation.

Everyone felt the sky was the limit for LeBron, but they could not envision how great he would actually be.

CHAPTER THREE

The "Fab Four" and Then Some More

Balls filled the net, sweaty bodies strained for rebounds, and sneakers scraped the hardwood. The sounds of shouts and the bounce of a basketball filled the arena. Practice was underway for the St. Vincent-St. Mary basketball team.

Suddenly, the door to the gymnasium opened. Some looked over to see the figure of LeBron James walking toward them.

It was late fall, and LeBron seemed happy to be coming out of the cold and into the warmth of the gym. He shook hands with some of the players. Then he wriggled out of his sweatpants into his basketball shorts.

James drives for a layup while playing for St. Vincent-St. Mary's.

He asked with a smile, "Can I play?"[1]

No response was necessary. LeBron effortlessly moved into the action of the game. He stole the ball from his opponent, cupped it in his hand, and glided through the air toward the basket.

Then came a backboard-rattling slam dunk that would do justice to any NBA player! However, this was just a high school freshman barely fifteen years old.

Watching in wonder was Keith Dambrot, the basketball coach at St. Vincent-St. Mary High School.

He was very much aware of LeBron's extraordinary talents. Dambrot had coached him and his buddies in various clinics around town when they

THE "FAB FOUR"

LeBron James, Dru Joyce III, Sian Cotton, and Willie McGee made up the "Fab Four" at St. Vincent-St. Mary High School.

Other "Fabs" included:

- Michigan Wolverines Chris Webber, Jalen Rose, Juwan Howard, Jimmy King, and Ray Jackson. They enjoyed great success in the nineties on the hardwood and were the inspiration for the "Fab Four" nickname for LeBron and the others.

- The original "Fab Four," the members of The Beatles rock band: John Lennon, Paul McCartney, George Harrison, and Ringo Starr.

were still AAU players. There usually wasn't a day when LeBron didn't show something new and unique and stunning with a basketball.

Having LeBron on his high school team was even more stunning for Dambrot. He never thought LeBron would decide to come to little St. Vincent-St. Mary. After all, he had so many big-name basketball schools in the Akron area from which to choose.

And Dambrot certainly didn't think he would get LeBron in a package deal with his three basketball-playing buddies. They called themselves the "Fab Four"—LeBron, Dru Joyce III, Sian Cotton, and Willie McGee.

The foursome had taken a page from the onetime spectacular "Fab Five" that had played for four years at Michigan. LeBron and his friends had been successful in AAU play. They so enjoyed playing together that they had decided to stay together through their high school years, much like the "Fab Five" had done at Michigan.

TAKING CHARGE

Although his basketball play as a freshman could be inconsistent, LeBron was a marvel to watch with his natural all-around abilities. LeBron could have a 25-point night or an 8-point night. Either way, he somehow managed to make a huge impact on a game. LeBron turned heads with dynamic dunks that shook the boards and brilliant passes that set up easy baskets for his teammates.

Even as a freshman, LeBron was starting to take charge of things on the basketball court. Dambrot was already regarding him as a unique player and giving him more responsibility with each game. LeBron had an instinctive genius for basketball with an ability to "see" the court better than most anyone else—that was his true talent.

The Irish won their opener as LeBron scored a modest 15 points. Game after game, they continued to win.

At the end of the season, the St. Vincent-St. Mary Fighting Irish were undefeated and in the Division III state championship game against Jamestown Greenview High School.

LeBron took charge. He scored 25 points, grabbed 9 rebounds, and assisted on 4 baskets to lead the Irish. The final score was St. Vincent-St. Mary 73, Jamestown Greenview 55.

The Irish finished with a 27–0 record and the state title in their division.

DID YOU KNOW?

St. Vincent-St. Mary High School had won just one boys' state basketball title (1984) before LeBron arrived. With LeBron on the team, the Fighting Irish won three state titles in four years (2000, 2001, and 2003).

James gets around the defense in a March 2003 game in Akron.

LeBron had averaged 18 points and 6 rebounds a game in his freshman season and had led his team to the state championship. How could he ever top that?

The answer came in LeBron's sophomore season. The Irish sprinted out to a 9–0 record before meeting powerful Oak Hill Academy from Virginia. Oak Hill was the number one-ranked high school team in the country.

There was enough interest in the game to have it played in Ohio State's arena in Columbus. Some 10,000 fans packed the building, along with a larger than normal media crowd. Even some NBA scouts were there.

LeBron had his best game as a high school player. He scored 33 points. However, the Irish fell short by one, losing 79–78 to the eventual national high school champions.

More than anything, the close game showed how good St. Vincent-St. Mary could really be. The Irish had played the number one-ranked high school basketball team in the country to a virtual standstill.

The Irish won the remainder of their games— including seven in the playoffs. They finished with a 26–1 record, including a 63–53 win against Casstown Miami East in the state title game.

For the second straight season, LeBron was named the tourney's Most Valuable Player and was selected for the all-state team.

In two years, LeBron and his team had earned two state titles. But that wasn't all Lebron did. Averaging 25.2 points, 7.2 rebounds, 5.8 assists, and 3.8 steals, LeBron became the first sophomore to receive Ohio's Mr. Basketball Award honoring the top high school player in the state.

Later, LeBron picked up another first when he was named to the *USA Today* All-America first team. No high school sophomore had ever done that before.

LeBron's football skills weren't ignored, either. In that sport, he was named first-team all-state as a wide receiver.

NATIONAL SCENE

However, it was his basketball skills that started to bring national attention to LeBron, particularly after the dramatic performance against Oak Hill. Along with recognition from *USA Today*, he was receiving attention from prominent national magazines.

DID YOU KNOW?

LeBron played high school football through his junior year and helped lead the Fighting Irish to the state semis his sophomore year.

With LeBron as the centerpiece, the St. Vincent-St. Mary basketball team became a big draw in the area. In order to accommodate a growing fan base, the Irish had moved some of their home games to the nearby University of Akron gym that seated about

6,000. And they were selling season tickets, which was unheard of for high school basketball games.

After his sophomore season, LeBron went to summer basketball camps. This is where elite high school players try to measure their skills against other top players in the country. They also try to catch the eye of college recruiters—and, in some cases, NBA scouts.

After his freshman year, LeBron had played in the prestigious Five-Star camp run by top basketball man Howard Garfinkel. A veteran who had seen it all, Garfinkel had praised LeBron to the skies. "I've never seen anything quite like it," he said after watching LeBron play.[2]

Now, after his sophomore year, LeBron headed for Colorado Springs, Colorado. There he competed in USA Basketball's Youth Development Festival featuring forty of the country's top high school players

WOULD YOU LIKE FRIES WITH THAT?

At the 2003 McDonald's All American High School Basketball Game, LeBron won the MVP award. He scored 27 points while pulling in 7 rebounds, picked up 7 assists, and helped the East team capture a 122–107 win. He was also the MVP of the EA Sports Roundball Classic and the Jordan Capital Classic.

James rushes toward the basket against Zanesville February 14, 2003.

in a four-day tournament. No surprise, LeBron led everyone in scoring with a 24-point average.

Then, LeBron went on to the Adidas ABCD Camp in Teaneck, New Jersey, for another challenge. Everyone was interested in seeing how LeBron would do against Lenny Cooke, a six-foot six-inch forward from Brooklyn, New York, widely regarded as one of the top seniors in the country. The match-up of their teams was the talk of basketball's inner circles.

"It seemed as if all week people were hyping it up like it was the Game of the Century," LeBron said. "I just wanted to give everyone a good show."[3]

He did, outscoring Cooke 24–9. More important, LeBron's team won 85–83 when he made a running three-pointer at the buzzer.

NBA scouts were impressed.

"He's the best high school player I've ever seen," one scout said of LeBron. "He's so explosive and versatile, and he has a great feel for the game. The guy is just a freak."[4]

PRO QUALITY

NBA-ready—that's what people were already starting to say about LeBron.

There had been high school players, such as Kobe Bryant and Kevin Garnett, who had made the jump from high school to the pros successfully. But they had at least graduated from high school. LeBron was

James laughs as he grabs his own rebound off a missed dunk during a game against Walsh Jesuit in Akron January 24, 2003.

just going into his junior year, and there was already talk that he would be leaving for the NBA.

Would he be the first to make the jump as a junior? LeBron shot down those rumors.

ST. VINCENT-ST. MARY ATHLETIC CHAMPIONSHIPS

Football: 1972, 1981, 1982, 1988

Girls Basketball: 1980, 1981, 1995

Boys Basketball: 1984, 2000, 2001, 2003

Baseball: 1986, 1989

Softball: 1979, 1984

Wrestling: 2001

Individual Basketball: 1972, 1979, 1981, 2001(3), 2002, 2003

Individual Cross Country: 2001, 2002, 2003

Individual Track: The 3200 in 2002 and 2003; the 4 x 800
    meter relay in 2005

"It's not going to happen," LeBron said. "I'm not going to give it any thought. I have friends here, and I'm not going to leave them. I'm going to graduate with my class and see what happens."[5]

But first there were still some goals for LeBron to reach in high school, such as another state championship or even a national championship.

Could he and his Irish teammates actually win the national title?

CHAPTER FOUR

That Championship Season

It was called the "Game of the Season." More than 11,000 fans, some paying as much as $75 a ticket, packed Cleveland State's Convocation Center.

Nearly a hundred members of the media from all across the country were on hand. There were also several NBA scouts and many professional athletes.

And it was televised nationally by ESPN.

Was this an NBA game? No, it was a high school game. But this one was special, matching the number one high school player in America against the number one team: LeBron James against Oak Hill Academy.

Of course, LeBron wasn't the only one playing for

St. Vincent-St. Mary High School, but he was by far the most talked about high school player in 2002.

Now a seventeen-year-old senior, he was expected to skip college and jump directly to the NBA.

Few high school players in history had generated as much interest as LeBron or as much praise.

"He's the best high school player that I've ever seen," said one NBA scout. "He's better than Kobe Bryant, Kevin Garnett, all of them."[1]

The clash with Oak Hill on December 12, 2002, was officially billed as the "Futures Game." People were talking about it months in advance, thanks to a press conference held in October by St. Vincent-St. Mary.

"This is unbelievable," said Dru Joyce III, whose father, Dru Joyce II, was now coaching the team. "We've played together since we were in the fourth grade and we always knew what we wanted to accomplish. But playing on ESPN on national TV, this is wild. And I love that we're playing Oak Hill because the last two years they got us."[2]

Oak Hill was a powerhouse from Virginia that had been turning out college and NBA players and national championships on a regular basis. The Warriors had at least five players on their roster heading to NCAA Division I colleges. They also had players from seven states.

They had won *USA Today*'s national title two times

James gets fired up in a game against Oak Hill Academy of Virginia.

in the previous four seasons. They had also beaten St. Vincent-St. Mary 79–78 in LeBron's sophomore year and 72–68 when LeBron was a junior.

BRINGING IT HOME

The 2002–03 season was get-even time for LeBron. Not only did he hope to finally defeat Oak Hill, but he wanted to bring the Irish back to the top of Ohio prep basketball. After two straight state titles, the Irish failed to win in 2001–02, LeBron's junior year. It was a major disappointment for LeBron.

To show how serious he was about basketball in his senior year, he even gave up football, his "first love."[3] As a junior, he had led the Irish football team to the state semifinals in the post-season playoffs with his great pass-catching ability. But while NFL teams considered LeBron a prime football prospect, LeBron's main focus as a senior was basketball.

Along with the state title, LeBron had another goal in mind: the national championship.

The talent was there to do it—and now for seniors LeBron James, Dru Joyce III, Sian Cotton, Willie McGee, and Romeo Travis, this was the final chance for them to win the championship wearing the green and gold of St. Vincent-St. Mary basketball. A victory against Oak Hill would give them a good measuring stick of their chances.

Less than a week before the Oak Hill game, the

IMPRESSIONS OF LEBRON AGAINST OAK HILL

"I came here with high expectations," said Hall of Famer Bill Walton, who asked ESPN2 if he could broadcast the game so he could get an up-close look at LeBron. "I'm leaving more impressed than I could have ever believed. This guy has the complete package. What I saw tonight was a special basketball player. It was an eye-opening experience for me."

Irish were in fine form. They buried Chicago Julian 75–50 in the "Challenge of Champions" game at the University of Akron's Rhodes Arena.

For a change, LeBron did not lead his team in scoring. But he did show other aspects of his game that made him such a great player.

"My game is to pass first and score second," LeBron said. "I told myself I was going to rebound and get my team some open shots. I'll do anything I need to do to help the team win. But I'll tell you, Thursday I'll turn it up."[4]

LeBron referred to the clash with Oak Hill just five days away.

There was an animated, noisy crowd of 11,523 at the Convocation Center to watch the battle of undefeated high school giants. It had the feel of an

NBA game, with such big names as Dick Vitale and Bill Walton doing the TV commentary for ESPN.

It was the first time in thirteen years that ESPN had televised a regular-season high school basketball game. The Goodyear blimp was also there, overhead for the first time at a high school basketball game in its 77 years in the air.

"I hope Kobe is watching," LeBron said, referring to the Los Angeles Lakers' Kobe Bryant, who had made the leap from high school to the NBA.[5]

LeBron enjoyed playing the role of the superstar and liked being the center of attention. After all, he had been doing it for several years now.

"I love it!" he said. "I want all of the spotlight. I'm not being selfish, because if I'm in the spotlight, my team is in the spotlight."[6]

With all eyes on LeBron, he struggled early. He clanked long jump shots off the rim a few times. Oak Hill jumped to a 10–3 lead.

LeBron was frustrated. He ripped out his mouthpiece. He threw his hands up. He motioned for support from the fans.

"Usually when we come out, two-thirds of the crowd is against us," said LeBron, referring to the many arenas the Irish visit across the country. "Tonight they were with us. There was a vibe."[7]

But even with that "vibe," LeBron's shots were not falling the way he wanted. Irish coach Dru Joyce ll pulled LeBron aside.

Forget about taking long perimeter shots, the coach advised LeBron. Take your game inside.

LeBron did. All of a sudden, he was making powerful dunk shots and easy layups.

At the half, LeBron had 13 points and St. Vincent-St. Mary had a 30–25 lead.

It was still a close game, too close to separate the two powers at that point. But LeBron wasn't going to let the Irish lose a third straight game to this team.

LEBRON, BY THE NUMBERS, AGAINST OAK HILL

Points: 31

Rebounds: 13

Attendance at the Convocation Center to watch the game: 11,523

Number of years the Goodyear blimp has been around (at game-time): 77

Number of high school basketball games the Goodyear blimp attended (at game-time): 1 (this one)

"I got the troops rallied and said, 'We can't let this happen. We have to go to work here,'" Lebron said.[8]

In the second half, that's just what the Irish did, led by their star. LeBron began connecting with his jumper. Suddenly he couldn't miss from the outside. His three-pointers sparked the Irish to a big lead and helped them withstand a late flurry by the Warriors.

The Irish held their usually high-scoring opponents to just 2 points in the fourth quarter, and

LeBron pretty much did what he wanted on the offensive end.

He finished with 31 points and 13 rebounds as St. Vincent-St. Mary crushed Oak Hill by a stunning 65–45 score.

It was a statement game for both LeBron and his team. Oak Hill coach Steve Smith said James' effort made the Irish the better team that night.

Other coaches felt the same way as the Irish outmatched other top high school teams around the country and climbed in the *USA Today* Super 25 high school basketball poll.

It seemed LeBron was on a one-man mission. And it seemed just about everyone wanted to see him. There were sold-out games everywhere the Irish played.

In Philadelphia, the Irish faced Strawberry Mansion and its superstar player, Maureece Rice. LeBron tallied 26 points, 8 rebounds, and 5 assists as the Irish won, 85–47.

In Columbus, Ohio, LeBron scored 27 points to lead the Irish to victory against Columbus Brookhaven 67–62 in overtime.

In Los Angeles, the Irish defeated Santa Ana Mater Dei 64–58 at UCLA's packed Pauley Pavilion. LeBron poured in 21 points and had 6 assists and 3 blocked shots.

It was the eighth straight victory for the undefeated Irish, and now they turned their attention to the *USA Today* poll.

"We've been chasing the goal for a national championship," LeBron said. "Hopefully when the poll comes out, we'll be number one. We are one of the hottest teams in America."[9]

Number one it was!

"It's good that we're number one," said Dru Joyce II, who had replaced Keith Dambrot that season as head coach at St. Vincent-St. Mary. "We've been playing well to beat some good teams, but we want to be number one with that last ranking. We need to get better every game to do that."[10]

James drives to the basket at Pauley Pavilion in Los Angeles in 2003.

The so-called "LeBron James Tour" continued to gather steam when the Irish rolled into Greensboro to play Winston-Salem Reynolds, a team that had won three straight North Carolina high school championships.

By then it was pretty much a foregone conclusion LeBron would be going professional after his senior year. A crowd of 16,200 at the Greensboro Coliseum cheered when the announcer said at the start of the game: "Let's welcome LeBron James to Greensboro! Good luck in the NBA next year, LeBron."[11]

Then LeBron put on an NBA-type performance with 32 points as the Irish crushed their opponents, 85–56.

NEGATIVE ATTENTION

It seemed that nothing could stop LeBron and his teammates from winning the national title—nothing, that is, except a couple of controversies.

Controversy number one was the Hummer.

One day LeBron pulled up to school in a shiny new platinum-colored vehicle. Students were impressed. It wasn't something they expected to see in the parking lot. It happened to be a Hummer—an expensive SUV valued between $50,000 and $80,000.

The *Cleveland Plain Dealer* reported it had the words "King James" printed on the front seat headrests and contained several television sets inside its roomy interior. The newspaper said the SUV was purchased from a car dealership in Los Angeles that sold luxury automobiles to professional athletes.

James puts up a shot against Detroit Redford January 12, 2003.

LeBron told his friends that the SUV was a gift from his mother for his eighteenth birthday.

There is nothing unlawful about a mother giving a birthday present to her son. But in LeBron's case, it caused heads to turn and sparked headlines in the newspapers.

As the number one high school basketball player in the country, he was constantly being watched. A brand-new luxury vehicle suddenly sitting in front of his house was cause for some suspicion. Where did Gloria James, a onetime welfare recipient, get all that money to buy an SUV?

She said that she had obtained a bank loan to pay for the Hummer. Nevertheless, the Ohio High School Athletic Association (OHSAA) investigated the situation. The OHSAA wanted to make sure that there was no evidence of wrongdoing, that the gift did not violate any state bylaws for amateur athletes. Gloria James supplied the association with the loan papers.

Finally, after two weeks of investigation, the OHSAA ruled no regulations had been violated. LeBron's amateur status as an athlete remained intact.

Before St. Vincent-St. Mary's final home game of the season, LeBron parked his Hummer right outside the school's gym doors so that all the students would be able to check it out.

That night, St. Vincent-St. Mary beat Akron-Buchtel 82–71. LeBron scored 25 points and added 15 rebounds and 8 assists. However, St. Vincent-St. Mary seemed sluggish at times—and coach Dru Joyce II felt the Hummer episode had something to do with it.

"It's not a major distraction," he said. "But let's face it, when something like this is going on, no matter how much you try to keep it from affecting you, it's still there. LeBron is newsworthy. If he breathes too hard it's going to be in the newspaper."[12]

Controversy number two involved the jerseys.

Less than a week after LeBron was cleared in the Hummer incident, he was the subject of another headline-making story. This time, newspapers reported that

KEEPING HIS COOL

When the Ohio High School Athletic Association began looking into the Hummer LeBron James was driving, he handled it as well as could be expected. During the investigation, before a game against Mentor, LeBron playfully drove a remote control Hummer around the gym floor and then proceeded to hit 19 of 25 shots, including a school record 11 three-pointers, on his way to another school record 50 points. And he didn't even play past the 6:27 mark of the Fighting Irish's 92–56 win. "I was in the zone," he said after the game. "When I'm in the zone, there's nothing anybody can do. I don't need to show anybody anything. I got the whole package."

James shoots from half court at the end of a quarter.

LeBron had accepted a gift of two vintage "throwback" jerseys from a Cleveland clothing store.

The jerseys—one of basketball star Wes Unseld and the other of football star Gale Sayers—were worth more than $800 combined. The owner of the store had given LeBron the jerseys as a gift in exchange for his autograph.

That was a no-no as far as the OHSAA was concerned. Amateur athletes are not allowed to accept such gifts. A high school athlete is prohibited from taking advantage of his athletic fame, said OHSAA commissioner Clair Muscaro. The association ruled LeBron ineligible for accepting the gift. In addition, the OHSAA ruled that LeBron's team would have to forfeit its victory against Buchtel High School and reduce its record to 13–1.

The season went on without LeBron. Minus their star player, the Irish struggled to beat Canton McKinley 63–62.

Meanwhile, LeBron took his battle to the courts to regain his eligibility.

Suddenly, he received good news! LeBron was back in action after a judge cleared the way with a temporary restraining order against the OHSAA.

Flashbulbs popped and a sellout crowd of 8,500 cheered as LeBron took the court with his teammates to face Westchester High, the seventh-ranked team in the country. The game against Westchester was part of an event called the Prime Time Shootout, which was held in Trenton, New Jersey.

LeBron's comeback had the atmosphere of an NBA playoff game. It was attended by 140 reporters, including some from as far away as Japan. Tickets were being scalped for as much as $2,500.

LeBron didn't waste any time, scoring on an 18-footer with his first attempt. By the end of the game, he had racked up a career-high 52 points. St. Vincent-St. Mary easily beat Westchester, 78–52. All by himself, LeBron had matched the scoring of the entire Westchester team!

"This court, this basketball court, is like my house," LeBron said. "I think missing a game last week gave me a little more motivation."[13]

BACK ON THE COURT

By the time the legal problems were settled, LeBron would miss one more game. But he was available for the playoffs. As expected, the Irish advanced to the Division II state championship game. Their opponent was Kettering Alter.

The title game was played before a state record crowd of 18,454 at the Value City Arena on the Ohio State University campus in Columbus. It marked the first time the arena was sold out for a state basketball game.

Before the contest, LeBron walked over to the St.

James drives the baseline past the Kettering defense during the Division II Finals March 22, 2003, in Columbus, Ohio.

Vincent-St. Mary student section holding his finger up in the air for "Number One." That's what the Irish were after a 40–36 victory that earned them their third state championship in four years. LeBron led the way with 25 points and 11 rebounds.

James plays in the McDonald's All American High School Game.

The fans were awed by James' variety of dunks, according to the *Toronto Star.*

The Irish completed their 2002–03 season with a 25–1 record. It would have been 26–0, except for the forfeit to Buchtel.

Even with the forfeit, LeBron expressed only joy with the season. He had good reason to be happy. He had averaged 31.6 points, 9.6 rebounds, 4.6 assists, and 3.4 steals for the season.

The Irish had made history as the first team in Ohio to appear in four consecutive state championship games.

"These guys have to go down as one of the greatest teams in Ohio high school history, if not the greatest," said Irish coach Dru Joyce II. "Considering all the scrutiny and adversity we faced day in and day out, you've got to applaud this team."[14]

The Irish soon added the national championship, capping LeBron's spectacular senior year.

During that time, no one beat the Irish on the court as they traveled from one end of the country to the other. They played in Los Angeles, Pittsburgh, Philadelphia, Trenton, Greensboro, Columbus, and Dayton, Ohio. They had traveled more than 15,000 miles, not unlike an NBA team.

LeBron put on more mileage in post-season all-star games.

First he participated in the McDonald's All

DID YOU KNOW?
The McDonald's All American High School Basketball Game started in 1978, and since that time more than $3 million has been raised for various charities. In addition to LeBron James, Michael Jordan, Magic Johnson, Kevin Garnett, Carmelo Anthony, J.J. Redick (Duke), Chris Paul, and Dee Brown (Illinois) all have played in the game.

American High School Game at Cleveland's Gund Arena. The place was packed—18,728 fans on hand to see the country's top high school basketball talent with most eyes focused on local hero LeBron James.

LeBron didn't disappoint the fans. He opened with a dunk 35 seconds into the game, then hit a pair of free throws, and soon set up Charlie Villanueva for two dunks. With 4 points, 3 assists, and a steal in the first five minutes, LeBron had a hand in 10 of the East team's initial 16 points.

By the time the game was done, LeBron had chalked up 27 points, 7 assists, 7 rebounds, 2 steals, and one blocked shot to stand head and shoulders above his fellow all-stars.

LeBron also made appearances in the EA Sports Roundball Classic in Chicago and the Jordan Capital Classic at the MCI Center in Washington, D.C.

The audience at the MCI Center was filled with

celebrities—Jordan, filmmaker Spike Lee, football star Warren Sapp, and rapper Bow Wow among them.

They watched the high-flying LeBron win the Most Valuable Player trophy with one of his best games of the year: 34 points, 12 rebounds, and 6 assists.

LeBron had delivered in spectacular style. The only thing he couldn't do was produce a victory for his "Silver" team against the "Black" team. It wasn't the worst thing, in LeBron's mind.

"If I finished my career with a loss at St. Vincent-St. Mary, I would be upset," he said, thinking back to the Ohio state championship game against Kettering Alter. "I'm two and one in these [all-star games]."[15]

It was only a matter of time before LeBron cashed in as a pro. He would be an instant millionaire. Big-time sneaker companies such as Nike and Adidas were battling to sign him to a fat endorsement contract.

When he announced at the end of the season that he was entering the NBA Draft, no one was surprised.

With all the traveling he had done in the last year, LeBron couldn't wait for his next stop: the NBA.

CHAPTER FIVE

Rookie Season

LeBron James stood in the lunch line waiting for his slices of pizza. It was one day after the Cleveland Cavaliers revealed they would make him the number one pick in the NBA Draft; yet he received no special favors.

Although he was a national celebrity, none of his classmates offered to let James move to the head of the line in the school cafeteria. None of his teachers allowed him to cut class. He still had homework to do.

With his high status in the draft and growing fame, it was a celebratory time in the James household. At school, it was just business as usual.

And LeBron liked it that way.

"LeBron still enjoys being a kid," said Irish football coach Jay Brophy. "Coming to school is probably the closest thing he has to normalcy."[1]

NBA commissioner David Stern congratulates James at the draft.

James models his new line of Nike sneakers.

At the age of eighteen, James was already one of the richest people in America with a $90 million sneaker deal that he signed with Nike. It wouldn't prove to be his only endorsement contract. And he would be making millions more once he signed with the Cavaliers.

The Cavaliers were eager to get James into the fold. One of the worst teams in the NBA for many years, they knew he could only make them better.

They certainly couldn't do much worse than the 2002–03 season. They had managed to win only 17 times in 82 games. It continued a trend of bad teams in Cleveland over the years.

Though James didn't guarantee a championship, he did promise the Cavaliers would be a better team than they were the last year.

But how much? That was the question.

Imagine the stress on a teenager who was carrying the hopes of an NBA franchise on his shoulders. Imagine being called the "Franchise."

"I know I'm a marked man," James said, "but I just have to go out there and play hard and play strong and help my teammates every night."[2]

James would also help the Cavs at the box office. Everywhere he had played, he usually filled the building.

And it was no different in the NBA's summer league when he officially stepped on a pro court for the first time. It was merely an exhibition game between the Cavaliers and the Orlando Magic. Yet an

61

electric crowd of 15,123, many of the fans wearing giveaway LeBron James jerseys, and nearly two hundred media representatives made it seem more like a playoff game.

James thrilled the crowd with some spectacular dunks as his team won the practice game.

"I like playing in front of big crowds," he said. "I like the stage. I think I play a lot better. My crowds last year in high school were bigger than the Cavs'."[3]

There hadn't been this much excitement in the NBA since Larry Bird and Magic Johnson entered in 1979 and revitalized the league. But they had long since retired, as had Michael Jordan.

The NBA was looking for another marquee player to capture the imagination of the fans. Would LeBron James be the one?

There was one big thing James had in common with Bird and Johnson. He enjoyed sharing the ball with teammates.

In his first pre-season game, against the Detroit Pistons, James made a play that made everyone sit up and take notice. On a fast break, Darius Miles passed the ball to James at the key. Without looking, he slipped a push pass to Ricky Davis, who scored two points!

"I saw Bird and Magic do that," Cavaliers general manager Jim Paxson said. "You can't teach that. That's a gift."[4]

Paxson continued to be impressed, as did the rest of the basketball world, as James smoothly made the transition to the NBA.

"He's wise beyond his years," said NBA Hall of Famer Jerry West. "He's got special tools. He'll have nights where he won't shoot well, but his total game makes him special."[5]

ADVICE FROM MALONE

The night before the opening game of the 2003–04 season, James had dinner with NBA Hall of Famer Moses Malone. Many years before, Malone had been the first big-time high school player to make the jump to the NBA.

Malone advised James on how to handle first-game jitters: "Stay focused and just compete. Don't back down from anybody."

"I've been hearing that a lot," James said, "but when you hear it from one of the greats, it makes it sound even better."[6]

MOSES MALONE: THE FIRST TO MAKE THE JUMP

Long before LeBron James became the latest prep star to go straight to the NBA, Moses Malone was the first player to take that plunge. How does James compare with Malone? In 1975, at the age of nineteen, Malone played in 83 games and scored 1,557 points. James, at the same age, played in 79 games and scored 1,654 points.

LeBron James prepares to take a shot.

His 25-point, 9-assist, 6-rebound performance against Sacramento showed James took the advice to heart. He followed that with 21 points, 12 rebounds, and 8 assists against Phoenix. Against Portland, he had an off night but did contribute 6 assists.

But his overall performance while playing three games in four nights was impressive for a rookie opening a season. The only thing he didn't do was bring his team a win on the 5,000-mile swing out west.

He was quickly learning what life would be like for him in the pros—exhausting travel days, bumping around in airports, constantly being asked for interviews and autographs. And James would always sign for the kids—no matter how tired he was or the time of day.

When the Cavaliers arrived at their hotel in Phoenix at 3 a.m., there were several autograph seekers waiting for him in the lobby.

Everywhere James went, fans were sure to follow. On one visit to Philadelphia, the Cavaliers were getting off their bus. They were at the bottom of a loading dock underneath the arena when fans from above dropped down jerseys on a rope for James to sign.

"It's crazy, but it's a dream come true," James said of the constant attention.[7]

But he still faced huge challenges trying to make the Cavaliers respectable. They were struggling in the early part of the 2003–04 season. They'd won only

"He was in the game on the bench."

—Coach Silas

two of their first seven games when the Philadelphia 76ers came to Cleveland.

The 76ers, one of the best teams in the league, had always given the Cavaliers trouble. Since 1999, the Cavs had lost to the 76ers 16 straight times.

A sellout crowd filled Gund Arena to see what the Cavs could do this time with James in the lineup.

The Cleveland fans cheered wildly as James put on a display of his various skills—monster dunks, light-fingered jump shots, and thread-needle passes.

By the end of regulation, the teams were tied. The Cleveland fans were being treated to something unusual: a tight game at home against a quality opponent.

The game stayed just as tight in overtime. Then, Zydrunas Ilgauskas scored to give the Cavs a 90–86 lead. The 76ers closed within 90–88 and had the ball with 11 seconds left.

The 76ers drew up a plan to get shooting specialist Kyle Korver free for a 15-foot shot from the baseline. The plan worked—until he tried to get off the shot.

Out of nowhere came James. He flashed in front of Korver, leaped into the air, and swatted the shot into the seats.

The Cavaliers held on for a 91–88 victory.

MAINTAINING GREATNESS

"Little by little, it is coming for us," Cleveland coach Paul Silas said. "It reinforces that we can win."[8]

This was far from a one-man team. But in order for the Cavs to win, James had to be at the top of his game. Could an eighteen-year-old rookie be great every night?

Early in December, the Cavaliers were on the West Coast to play the Los Angeles Clippers. Hollywood celebrities and sports stars had turned out to see the young star. Billy Crystal, Brandy, and Serena Williams were waiting to be electrified by LeBron James.

They weren't. He had an ordinary night. Actually, it proved far less than ordinary. He only made 2 of 13 shots and finished with a season-low 4 points. He was pulled from the game with more than seven minutes remaining by Coach Silas.

It was the first time in his career that James had been benched.

"I'm not upset," he said after the 90–80 loss to the Clippers. "The coach makes decisions. I know most of the time I'm going to be in there."[9]

But while on the bench, James did something that Silas appreciated: Instead of sulking, he waved a towel and cheered on his teammates.

"I liked that," Silas said. "He was in the game on the bench."[10]

James fends off Chicago defenders during a December 2003 game.

The media came down hard on James, though.

"James played like the growing rookie that he is, yet grumbling fans wanted the 'Magic' that he was supposed to be," said the *Los Angeles Times*.[11]

Later in the month, the Cavaliers visited Chicago for a game with the Bulls. The night before, the Cavaliers had snapped a 34-game road losing streak—the second longest in NBA history—with a victory at Philadelphia.

Now they had a chance to make it two in row in Chicago. Watching from a suite in the United Center was Michael Jordan, James' boyhood hero.

It was time for a Jordan-like performance.

James scored 32 points, including his team's final 14. In the fourth quarter, James outscored the entire Bulls team 15–14! He also handed out 10 assists, as the Cavaliers triumphed, 95–87.

"I feel I'm the leader of this team right now," James said. "They came to me and I helped them down the stretch."[12]

That would be repeated again and again as the season continued. At the halfway point, the Cavaliers already had more victories than they had tallied in the entire previous season. It was obvious no player was more responsible for that than James.

There was still a long way to go, but the Cavaliers were actually contenders for a playoff berth. That hadn't been the case in Cleveland for many years.

AN IMMEDIATE IMPACT

Cleveland Cavaliers' record 2002–03 season: 17–65

Cleveland Cavaliers' record 2003–04 season
(James' rookie year): 35–47

Cleveland Cavaliers' average home attendance 2002–03
season: 11,497

Cleveland Cavaliers' average home attendance 2003–04
season: 18,288

Cleveland Cavaliers' average home attendance 2004–05
season: 19,128 (sixth highest in the NBA)

WHO'S THE BEST?

There was another race shaping up in the NBA—between James and Carmelo Anthony for Rookie of the Year honors.

While James was getting most of the attention, Anthony was having an equally fine first season with the Denver Nuggets. James and Anthony knew each other from a high school rivalry. And Anthony had led Syracuse to the NCAA championship as a freshman before joining the pros.

While James was picked first in the NBA Draft, Anthony wasn't far behind at number three. When they faced each other in the NBA for the first time, more than 300 media members attended. The game ended in a 93–89 victory for Denver. Although Anthony won the scoring duel with 14 points to James' 7, the Cleveland rookie had 11 rebounds and 7 assists.

Their competition would heat up to fever pitch as the season wore on.

On December 13, James scored 37 points against the Boston Celtics. Two weeks later, Anthony scored 37 against the Houston Rockets.

On February 1, James scored 38 against the Washington Wizards. The next night, Anthony put up 39 against the Portland Trail Blazers.

Late in the season, James had 41 against the New Jersey Nets. A couple of nights later, Anthony matched it against the Seattle SuperSonics.

After the game, Anthony said: "I couldn't let LeBron get 41 without me getting 41. I talked to him about that."[13]

With one quarter of the NBA season remaining, James and Anthony were both scoring more than 20 points a game—the highest averages for rookies since Tim Duncan's 21.1 mark for San Antonio in 1997–98. James and Anthony also were breezing toward a record for teenagers in the NBA with their 20-plus averages. Kobe Bryant had set the mark with 15.4 in his second season with the Los Angeles Lakers.

James and Anthony not only put up great numbers, they also improved their respective teams after

James blocks a shot by Carmelo Anthony.

they had finished tied for the NBA's worst record at 17–65 in 2002–03.

With James leading the way in 2003–04, the Cavaliers jumped to 35–47, a difference of eighteen games in the win column. Anthony's Denver Nuggets improved by twenty-six games, to 43–39.

James also made an impact in other ways for the Cavs. He helped their average home attendance rise from 11,497 to 18,288.

"He never hit a wall [of fatigue]. He stayed humble. He didn't antagonize other players. No question about it, he can be one of the best ever."

—Coach Silas

In addition, he made an impact on the league. His wine-and-gold number 23 Cavaliers jersey was the hottest seller in the NBA.

There was only one thing James couldn't do— lead his team to the playoffs. Despite their huge improvement, the Cavs finished ninth in their division, falling one spot short of a playoff berth.

But James had delivered on his promise to make the Cavaliers better.

NBA ROOKIE OF THE YEAR HISTORY

1952–53: Don Meineke, Fort Wayne

1953–54: Ray Felix, Baltimore

1954–55: Bob Pettit, Milwaukee

1955–56: Maurice Stokes, Rochester

1956–57: Tom Heinsohn, Boston

1957–58: Woody Sauldsberry, Philadelphia

1958–59: Elgin Baylor, Minneapolis

1959–60: Wilt Chamberlain, Philadelphia

1960–61: Oscar Robertson, Cincinnati

1961–62: Walt Bellamy, Chicago

1962–63: Terry Dischinger, Chicago

1963–64: Jerry Lucas, Cincinnati

1964–65: Willis Reed, New York

1965–66: Rick Barry, San Francisco

1966–67: Dave Bing, Detroit

1967–68: Earl Monroe, Baltimore

1968–69: Wes Unseld, Baltimore

1969–70: Kareem Abdul-Jabbar, Milwaukee

1970–71: Dave Cowens, Boston;
Geoff Petrie, Portland (tie)

1971–72: Sidney Wicks, Portland

1972–73: Bob McAdoo, Buffalo

1973–74: Ernie DiGregorio, Buffalo

1974–75: Keith Wilkes, Golden State

1975–76: Alvan Adams, Phoenix

1976–77: Adrian Dantley, Buffalo

1977–78: Walter Davis, Phoenix

1978–79: Phil Ford, Kansas City

1979–80: Larry Bird, Boston

1980–81: Darrell Griffith, Utah

1981–82: Buck Williams, New Jersey

1982–83: Terry Cummings, San Diego

1983–84: Ralph Sampson, Houston

1984–85: Michael Jordan, Chicago

1985–86: Patrick Ewing, New York

1986–87: Chuck Person, Indiana

1987–88: Mark Jackson, New York

1988–89: Mitch Richmond, Golden State

1989–90: David Robinson, San Antonio

1990–91: Derrick Coleman, New Jersey

1991–92: Larry Johnson, Charlotte

1992–93: Shaquille O'Neal, Orlando

1993–94: Chris Webber, Golden State

1994–95: Grant Hill, Detroit; Jason Kidd, Dallas (tie)

1995–96: Damon Stoudamire, Toronto

1996–97: Allen Iverson, Philadelphia

1997–98: Tim Duncan, San Antonio

1998–99: Vince Carter, Toronto

1999–2000: Elton Brand, Chicago:
　　　　　Steve Francis, Houston (tie)

2000–01: Mike Miller, Orlando

2001–02: Pau Gasol, Memphis

2002–03: Amare Stoudemire, Phoenix

2003–04: LeBron James, Cleveland

2004–05: Emeka Okafor, Charlotte Bobcats

2005–06: Chris Paul, New Orleans/Oklahoma City Hornets

2006–07: Brandon Roy, Portland Trail Blazers

> "He proved to all of us that he is up for a challenge. He exceeded all of our expectations and just kept raising the bar."
>
> —Cavaliers owner Gordon Gund, commenting on James after he won the Rookie of the Year Award

He had averaged more than 20 points, 5 assists, and 5 rebounds, only the third rookie in NBA history to do so. But that wasn't the only reason he felt he'd had a successful season.

"We doubled our win total, plus one," James said. "That was my main concern—that we get better from day one."[14]

One other accomplishment for him was that he was named Rookie of the Year. James beat out his friend Anthony for the prestigious award.

"He came on like gangbusters, didn't he?" Cavs coach Paul Silas said of James. "He never hit a wall [of fatigue]. He stayed humble. He didn't antagonize other players. No question about it, he can be one of the best ever."[15]

James and coach Paul Silas share a laugh during a press conference announcing James as the NBA Rookie of the Year.

CHAPTER SIX

James' Journey

Like a politician, LeBron James worked the room. But this was a basketball player, not a politician, and the "room" was Gund Arena in Cleveland, Ohio.

Long after his teammates had cleared out after the game, and many of the fans had left as well, James remained to sign autographs, lift gurgling babies in the air, and kiss middle-aged ladies.

In his first year with the Cavaliers, James had already won over fans with his extraordinary play. Now he was winning them over with his charm.

"He's been groomed for this," Silas said.[1]

James has taken it all in stride.

"People ask me how do I handle things so well," he said. "I'm just being myself.... A God-given talent on and off the court have set me up like this."[2]

James talks to media after dedicating a new community center gym.

James talks to kids about healthy lifestyles.

Just as easily as James made the transition from high school to the NBA, he has slipped into the role as the "face" of the Cavaliers' franchise. As such, he recognizes his responsibility to deal with the public and the media.

"His ability to channel the publicity in a positive direction has been impressive," said Rodney Knox, a spokesman for Nike. "I've been around Hall of Fame-type players like Joe Montana, Jerry Rice, Ronnie Lott. But to watch LeBron handle the same sort of stuff at his age . . . he's just been masterful."[3]

Young fans have always been James' top priority among his followers.

"I make sure I take care of the kids first, that's what I do," he said. "I'm a kid. If I see a kid, I'm going to try to spend as much time with him as I can. If I pass up a kid, it's not on purpose. When you're a pro, you're a role model whether you are a star or the last person on the bench. We're all part of that NBA logo. That puts everything in perspective."[4]

Winning over his teammates has come naturally, too.

"If he was a selfish kind of player, it wouldn't work," Silas said. "He looks to pass first, shoot second—which the great ones do."[5]

James has been compared to Magic Johnson in this regard. He gets as much fun out of setting up a teammate for a basket as he does scoring himself—maybe more.

> ## "He keeps his teammates involved. That he's willing to drive it at the end and kick it to a teammate, well, that's not like a second-year player."
>
> ### —Celtics coach Doc Rivers

Like Johnson, James has the ability to make his teammates better.

Early in his second season, the Cavaliers were playing the Boston Celtics. James drove the lane late in the game. Instead of taking the shot himself, which most players would, he dropped the ball off to center Ilgauskas for an easy score.

The basket put the Cavs in command. Then James raced back on defense and blocked a shot by the Celtics' Paul Pierce to clinch the victory for Cleveland.

"Forget the talent and the athletic ability, it's his maturity that's light years ahead," said Celtics coach Doc Rivers. "He keeps his teammates involved. That he's willing to drive it at the end and kick it to a teammate, well, that's not like a second-year player."[6]

This type of play is one of the reasons James has been compared to Oscar Robertson. Robertson was known for his "triple-doubles"—scoring in double figures in three categories in a game such as points, rebounds, and assists. Unbelievable as it seems, Robertson did this for an entire season! The Hall of Famer says that if anyone in the NBA could match that feat, it would be LeBron James.

At six feet eight inches, 240 pounds, and with the way he plays, James doesn't fit the description of any specific basketball position. He is regarded as a "swing man." That means he can fill the roles of any four positions on the floor when necessary: point guard directing the offense, shooting guard counted on to score points, power forward used mainly for rebounding, and small forward depended on mostly for scoring.

James has enough speed to bring the ball up the court for his team and enough strength and savvy to battle underneath the boards for rebounds. And he usually leads the Cavs in most categories each game.

James' consistency in his rookie year was all the more amazing because most first-year players in the NBA usually "hit the wall" at some point—they are overcome by the fatigue of the long and tiring 82-game season, and their performance drops off. James never experienced that because of his size and conditioning.

In high school, James had been a great practice player, according to his coach, Dru Joyce II. That hasn't changed since he joined the NBA.

"That's the only way it should be—you gotta be competitive," James says. "It doesn't matter what I'm doing—just playing cards, just playing video games, if it's playing horse, I don't want to lose."[7]

MUST BE THE SHOES

James isn't only a point-making machine in the NBA. He's a money-making machine for himself, his team, and his league.

His three-year rookie deal with the Cavaliers is worth about $13 million, with a club option for a fourth year totaling approximately $19 million. In addition, he has signed long-term endorsement deals worth more than $100 million, the larger portion from Nike.

NUMBER 23, MICHAEL JORDAN

James chose uniform number 23 because of his admiration of Michael Jordan. But did you know that during his basketball career, Jordan also wore number 45 (for 21 games in 1995, after coming back from his first retirement), number 9 (on the 1992 U.S. Olympic Dream Team), and number 12 (emergency uniform worn against the Orlando Magic in the 1990–91 season after the Bulls' uniforms had been stolen)?

A customer buys a pair of Nike LeBron James shoes just after midnight December 20, 2003, right when they first went on sale.

It is not surprising that James went with Nike. Michael Jordan's affiliation with the company might have helped to tip the balance.

Like Jordan, James has helped to fill arenas both at home and on the road. He has also helped the NBA's well-oiled marketing machine. His number 23 jersey became one of the hottest items at arena concession stands and in stores around the country. The NBA is also counting on James to revitalize the league, much as Jordan did, and Larry Bird and Magic Johnson before him.

KEEPING KIDS INVOLVED: PE2GO

PE2GO is a joint venture between Nike and the SPARK Programs of San Diego State University, which stands for "Sports, Play and Active Recreation for Kids." The program works to get kids moving and more physically active.

PE2GO is part of a broader community affairs program called NikeGO, focusing on children ages eight through fifteen across the United States. The program gives the following support to pilot schools:

• Customized curriculum for fourth- and fifth-grade teachers.

• Customized hands-on staff training to improve physical activity programs in the schools, to meet state/national standards, and to address the things that get in the way of physical education quantity and quality.

• Equipment worth more than $10,000.

More information can be found at www.nikego.com.

"It's really cool to go to different cities, see different fans and the reaction the fans give you on and off the court," James says. "You get away from home and you see people still wearing your jersey. That feels pretty good."[8]

James has given back generously, and not only by meeting and greeting his fans. He has teamed with Nike on a physical education program called PE2GO to help schools that have been hit hard by budget cuts. PE2GO provides these money-strapped schools with equipment and instructions for teachers to promote exercise programs.

"When I was in gym class I remember how much I loved it, and I don't want kids to lose out on things like kickball, basketball, and dodgeball," he said. "Even when I was in the fourth and fifth grades, phys ed was an important component in my life."[9]

James likes to help people, much like his favorite comic book character: Batman.

"I grew up reading comic books," he says. "I want my character to grow into a Batman–Bruce Wayne type, a regular guy who helps people and makes the world a better place."[10]

James has grown up fast. He was eighteen when he was made a first-round draft pick in the NBA and nineteen when he became a father. James so far refuses to share any information about his child with reporters.

James said, "I don't want to get into my personal

life, I'm just worrying about basketball right now."[11]

And he is expected to carry a whole league virtually by himself. He's expected to make the Cleveland Cavaliers better, make his teammates better, and eventually lead them to an NBA championship.

There is a lot of hype, but James has only set modest goals for himself. He just hopes to get better every year as a person and as a basketball player.

BATMAN

LeBron James says his favorite comic book character is Batman. Did you know that Batman has his own Web site? The address is www.batman.com.

CHAPTER SEVEN

Going for 50

I

t is nearly game time. The Cleveland Cavaliers are preparing to face the Toronto Raptors late in the 2004–05 season, and LeBron James is meeting with reporters.

He has just come off his worst shooting night of the year, a dismal 3-for-20 against the Philadelphia 76ers two nights before.

"Can you bounce back?" he is asked.

"I'll take care of that right now," he says.[1]

James is never short of confidence. But would he make up for his poor performance against the 76ers?

So far, the season had many more ups than downs for him. He was not bothered by the so-called "sophomore jinx" that sometimes affects players in their second year in the pros. Averaging more than 20 points a game, James had not had too many off

89

LEBRON JAMES ★ KING ON AND OFF THE COURT

nights. Now, the media was interested to see how he would react after his worst game of the season.

The media was also interested to see how the Cavaliers would play as a team. All of a sudden, they had gone into a tailspin and needed a big game from James to lift them.

From the opening tip-off in Toronto, everyone in the building could see that James was on his game.

He scored 16 points in the first quarter and 13 in the second—29 points in the first half!

Earlier in the season, James had scored a career-high 43 points against the Detroit Pistons. Could he possibly match that against the Raptors?

PROVING HIMSELF

Before the second half started, James took a seat on the press table.

He kidded with reporters: "I told you."[2]

The second half started, and there was no letup from James. He scored 9 points in the third quarter.

Then with 2:22 remaining in the fourth, James made a short bank shot from the left wing. It was point number 50, a rare achievement in the NBA.

That matched the Cavs' team record, scored by Walt Wesley on February 19, 1971, against Cincinnati.

But James was not finished. With 1:44 remaining, he hit a three-pointer to give him 18 points in the fourth quarter. He exploded with a run of six straight shots!

DID YOU KNOW?

LeBron James scoring 50 points at such a young age was quite an accomplishment, but will he ever make a run at the all-time single-game scoring record of 100 points in a game? On March 2, 1962, the Philadelphia Warriors' Wilt Chamberlain scored 100 points against the New York Knicks. While Chamberlain was a center, the most-ever points in a game for a non-center (also the second most all-time), came on January 22, 2006, when the Los Angeles Lakers' Kobe Bryant scored 81 points against the Toronto Raptors.

By the time the final buzzer sounded, James had shattered the team record by scoring 56 points!

At twenty years and 80 days old, James became the youngest player in NBA history to score 50 points, bettering the achievement of Rick Barry. Barry was twenty-one years, 261 days old when he set the record with 57 for San Francisco against the New York Knicks on December 14, 1965.

James had shot 18-for-36 from the field, including 6 three-pointers, and 14-of-15 from the foul line. He also had 10 rebounds and 5 assists while playing the full 48 minutes.

The only thing missing from his sensational night was a victory against the Raptors. The Cavaliers lost the game, 105–98.

RICK BARRY: FAST FACTS

- Inducted into the NBA Hall of Fame in 1987.
- Two-time All-State selection at Roselle Park (New Jersey) High School.
- Attended the University of Miami from 1961 to 1965 where he was an AP First-Team All-America selection in 1965, *The Sporting News* Second Team All-American in 1965, and led the nation in scoring with 37.4 points per game his senior year.
- Played in the ABA (Oakland Oaks, Washington Capitals, New York Nets) from 1968 to 1972.
- Played in the NBA (San Francisco/Golden State, Houston Rockets) 1965–67, 1972–79.
- NBA Rookie of the Year in 1966.
- Led the NBA in scoring in 1967 (35.6).
- Eight-time NBA All-Star.
- He was the only player to lead the NCAA, ABA, and NBA in scoring.

"It was probably the best game of my life," James said, "but it means nothing when you lose."[3]

It meant a lot to the people who watched the game. It wasn't only the number of points that he scored—it was the different ways he had scored them: backboard-rattling dunks, long arcing jump shots, and running three-pointers, some of them off balance. And he did a lot of the damage while being double-teamed by the Raptors.

James is fouled by Toronto's Matt Bonner.

DID YOU KNOW?

Michael Jordan scored 50 points in a game a remarkable 37 times in his career! His career high in points came against Cleveland, when on March 28, 1990, he scored 69 points in the Bulls' 117–103 overtime victory at Cleveland. The first time Jordan ever scored 50 points in a game was on April 20, 1986, when he scored 63 against Larry Bird and the Boston Celtics. He was twenty-three years old.

"A couple of those one-legged jumpers reminded me of another twenty-three I played against once or twice," said Raptors forward Jalen Rose, referring to all-time great Michael Jordan.[4]

Five different Raptor players tried to stop James at various times, to no avail. The Cavaliers' star went on to outscore the rest of his teammates 56–42!

"I thought he earned all 56," said Raptors coach Sam Mitchell. "I mean, he hit some fadeaway threes and shots, but he had two guys contesting him."[5]

After James' performance against the Raptors, and his history, it was only inevitable that comparisons were

YOUTH IS SERVED

LeBron James is doing it all, and he's doing it at a young age. Some of his accomplishments:

- 2004 NBA Rookie of the Year (youngest in NBA history).
- Youngest player in NBA history to record a triple-double.
- Youngest player in NBA history to score 50 points in a game.
- Youngest player in NBA history to reach 5,000 points, 1,000 rebounds, and 1,000 assists.

starting to be made with the NBA's all-time greats.

"He's going to set a lot more records, you know, if he develops," Silas said. "He was just on fire tonight. He was just amazing and it was great to see."[6]

CHAPTER EIGHT

The Beat Goes On

It was the eve of LeBron James' twentieth birthday, but he didn't feel like celebrating. Instead he sat glumly on the Cleveland Cavaliers' bench, his head covered by a towel. He looked like a dazed fighter who had just been revived after a knockout.

That was very nearly the case. James had been knocked down by a blow from the elbow of Houston's Dikembe Mutombo. The result was a fractured cheek.

James was moving across the lane when he was struck by Mutombo's elbow and suddenly found himself sprawled out on the court.

"I never saw him," Mutombo said. "The next thing I know, boom, he was lying on the floor."[1]

James grimaces after an injury December 29, 2004.

HAPPY BIRTHDAY

LeBron James' twenty-first birthday went better than his twentieth. Two days before he turned twenty-one, James threw a big birthday party at Cleveland's House of Blues. He had a private dinner party with 65 guests and then joined 1,000 of his closest friends for an all-out celebration. Proceeds from the evening's ticket sales were given to charity.

James was stunned and needed help to get to the Cavs' bench. He later went to the hospital for X-rays.

"It was one of the hardest hits I ever took," he said later. "I've never felt anything like that."[2]

He spent the entire second half of that game sitting on the bench.

A couple days later, he was ready to go back into action against the Charlotte Bobcats wearing a special mask to protect him from further injury. He was fitted with the mask in Cleveland, and then flew to Charlotte, North Carolina, to join his teammates.

"I feel a lot better," he said. "There's still a little pain, but that's nothing."[3]

Cavaliers coach Paul Silas said the decision to play had been left up to James.

"There's still a little bit of swelling, but it's down substantially," Silas said.[4]

If he was bothered by the injury or the mask, James didn't show it against the Bobcats.

With 6:03 left in the first quarter, he rattled the backboard with a dunk.

"You're all right! You're all right!" yelled his teammate Ira Newble.[5]

And he was. James shot 11 of 19 from the floor and added 8 rebounds and 6 assists to lead the Cavaliers over the Bobcats 94–83.

It was no less than James had been doing all season.

At the halfway mark of only his second year in the NBA, James was already in the running for the league's scoring title and Most Valuable Player award! And—another surprise—the Cavaliers were in the running for a playoff berth.

When James had first started in the NBA, there were expectations he would improve the Cavs. But few had expected him to improve them so quickly and so dramatically.

"He could be the best ever," Denver Nuggets coach George Karl said about him. "His maturity is the thing that is the most startling about him. His basketball sense has gotten him to where he is."[6]

OLYMPIC DREAMS

Basketball sense was the main reason coach Larry

Brown wanted James on his United States basketball team at the Olympics in the summer of 2004. Also, James was his most versatile player.

"He knows how to run every position," Brown said of James, who was the youngest male basketball player from the United States to participate in the Olympics since Spencer Haywood in 1968.[7]

One of James' Olympic highlights came midway through the second period against Greece: He led the Americans on an 11–0 run to give them a 12-point lead. James scored 8 of the points.

Another highlight: In the same game, James dove for a loose ball and came up with a valuable possession for Team USA. The 77–71 victory against Greece was one of the better moments for an American team that struggled throughout most of the Olympic tourney. The Americans missed out on the gold medal, settling for the bronze.

GETTING IT DONE

The Cavaliers had better luck as they began the 2004–05 season behind James' fast start.

"The thing that LeBron can do now that he couldn't do last year—he can take over a game," Silas said. "He can just say, 'Give me the ball and I'll get it done for you.'"[8]

For example, early in the season, the Cavs played the Phoenix Suns, one of the NBA's surprising powerhouses. In the fourth quarter, James outscored the entire Suns team all by himself, 17–14! The Cavaliers overcame a 19-point deficit and went on to beat the previously unbeaten Suns in overtime, 114–109.

James finished with 38 points, 10 rebounds, 6 assists, and 3 steals.

In another game, James scored 43 points to lead the Cavaliers to a 92–76 victory against the defending NBA champion Detroit Pistons.

"He's definitely the hardest guy in the league to guard," said Pistons forward Tayshaun Prince.[9]

Against the Chicago Bulls, James scored 26 points to become the youngest player in NBA history to reach the 2,000-point mark.

James' Olympic experience, even though limited, had served him well.

"I learned a lot of things," he said, "and I was able to transfer them to the games now."[10]

DID YOU KNOW?

Since 1936 when the United States first sent a men's basketball team to the Olympics, they have captured twelve gold medals, one silver medal, and two bronze medals. After helping lead the United States to a bronze medal in 2004, LeBron James has already committed to play again in 2008 in Beijing, China.

ALL-STAR

First, James participated in the Olympics. Then he was part of the NBA All-Star game, where he offered a highlight-reel dunk.

Shaquille O'Neal blocked a shot by Amare Stoudemire, grabbed the ball in the air, and shoveled it ahead to Allen Iverson on a fast break. Iverson, 40 feet from the basket, lofted an "alley-oop" pass high toward the rim. It looked like a bad pass, sailing over the heads of everyone.

But, wait! Before the ball flew out of bounds, James streaked in from the right side. Suddenly, he went up and grabbed the ball with one hand. With the same motion, he stuffed it through the basket for two points.

James' East team went on to beat the West 125–115.

CHAPTER NINE

A Gift for Cleveland and the League

James was getting used to winning in the NBA, as was his Cavaliers team. In late December, the Cavs had already won twenty-four games—seven more than in the entire season in the pre-LeBron James era two years before.

Even though they suddenly went into a nosedive late in the 2004–05 season, they were still competing for their first playoff berth since 1998. The late-season slide had cost Silas his job, but the Cavs were in the playoff battle right down to the final day of the season.

In an NBA commercial before the start of the

season, James made a New Year's resolution: average a triple-double for the entire year.

He did not do that, but his statistics were impressive, particularly for a second-year player. With one decisive game left in the 2004–05 season, James was averaging about 25 points, 7 rebounds, and 7 assists a game.

James needed another great game if the Cavaliers were to have any chance of making the playoffs. And still, a victory against Toronto on the last day of the season would not guarantee anything. The race with the New Jersey Nets for the final playoff spot in the East was that close.

So what did James do? He simply scored 27 points, grabbed 14 rebounds, and handed out 14 assists for his fourth triple-double of the season as the Cavaliers beat the Raptors in Toronto, 104–95.

Alas, one of James' greatest performances went to waste as the Nets won their game to squeeze past Cleveland into the playoffs.

"I just wanted to put us in a position to win," James said. "I did that. We needed some help, but we didn't get it."[1]

The Cavaliers, however, did finish with a winning record at 42–40 only two seasons after the team had gone 17–65. The difference was mostly LeBron James.

In only two years, he had made a dramatic impact on a team, a league, and a city. His gigantic image

James goes up for a shot after beating the Nets' defense.

towered over downtown Cleveland on a billboard 10 stories tall and 212 feet wide.

The Cavaliers' fans could only wonder what the future would bring for their team. They didn't have to wait long.

Prior to the 2005–06 season, the Cavaliers spent $150 million for some of the top free agents in the NBA. They signed Larry Hughes, Donyell Marshall, and Damon Jones and re-signed Zydrunas Ilgauskas. Under new coach Mike Brown, the Cavaliers suddenly had one of the most dangerous teams in the league.

James, supported by his new teammates, sparked the Cavaliers on an eight-game winning streak early in the season. Another historic first for LeBron: With 26 points against the Orlando Magic in an overtime 108–100 Cleveland victory, he became the youngest player in NBA history to reach 4,000 career points.

At 20 years and 318 days, LeBron snapped the record set by the Los Angeles Lakers' Kobe Bryant (21 years and 216 days).

"It couldn't happen to a better person," Brown said of James. "He's a great person, great leader, and I enjoy being around him. To be around when [the 4,000-point level] happened, is a tremendous feeling."[2]

In the off-season, James had worked on his outside shot. It paid off. In November, he averaged 28.4 points (along with 6.0 rebounds and 4.5 assists) and was named

ANOTHER MILESTONE

On January 21, 2006, James scored 51 points in the Cavs' 108–90 victory against the Utah Jazz at the Delta Center. In that game, he became the youngest player to score 5,000 points at 21 years, 22 days. Kobe Bryant scored his 5,000th career point at 22 years, 116 days. When James left the game late in the fourth quarter, he received an ovation from the Utah fans. "That was awesome," James said of the Delta Center crowd. "To have opposing fans cheer for you doesn't get any better than that. That was awesome to see."

the Eastern Conference's Player of the Month. The Cavs were off to a hot start, too, with a 10–4 record.

HELPING OTHERS

James was also putting up big numbers in assists off the court with his James Family Foundation. The foundation lends support in a variety of ways to needy families, particularly those with single parents. In the summer of 2005, the foundation donated 1,000 backpacks full of school supplies to youngsters in the Akron and Cleveland areas.

"Starting the school year with a pencil, paper, and something to put it in was one thing I made sure LeBron had every school year," said LeBron's mother, Gloria James, founder of the James Family Foundation. "Now we want to help others by providing those same things."[3]

GIVING BACK TO AKRON

Akron Mayor Don Plusquellic had this to say, on the occasion of the King for Kids Bike-a-thon: "Akron is so proud of LeBron James' achievements on and off the basketball court that we wanted youngsters from the city to be a part of his first charity fund-raiser." A special Children's Bike Ride will feature 200 youngsters who will be selected by administrators from Akron's Recreation Bureau and the Akron Metropolitan Housing Authority. To be selected, kids will have been active in programs at one of the city's 13 recreation centers or live in AMHA housing. All will have demonstrated good citizenship in their daily lives.

"LeBron has always had a special connection with kids, and he will continue to support and encourage them to succeed," said Bike-a-thon executive director Chris Dennis. "Because the Bike-a-thon is primarily benefiting youth and families in this community, it is very appropriate to get children involved in the ride with LeBron, especially those who may not ordinarily have the opportunity to do it."

James' good deeds in his community are well documented. In 2003, he funded a physical education program for kids in the Akron public school system called PE2GO. In 2004 he was on the scene to dedicate the first of ten basketball courts he was having refurbished in Akron.

And in 2005, he sponsored a King for Kids Bike-a-thon to promote physical fitness for kids. Several NBA stars were on hand for the race, which was run on some of the same west and north side streets of Akron where James grew up. And those were only a small part of James' charitable contributions to his community and elsewhere.

James greets children after dedicating two basketball courts in an Akron park.

"Our resident superstar is giving back to Akron," said Mayor Don Plusquellic.[4]

It was nothing that James hadn't been doing all along. "One of my goals is to put smiles on kids' faces," he said.[5]

BACK ON THE COURT

Meanwhile, James is also putting smiles on the faces of the Cavaliers' fans. James delivered the team's first playoff appearance in eight years at the end of the 2005-06 season. In the process, James helped the Cavaliers reach 50 wins in a season for the first time since 1992-93. Their 50-32 record ranked fourth in the Eastern Conference.

In his first playoff appearance ever, James didn't disappoint. He led the Cavaliers to a victory in their first-round series, four games to two over the Washington Wizards. James made game-winning baskets in two of those victories and averaged 35.6 points per game. In the second round, the Cavaliers pushed the powerful Detroit Pistons to seven games before losing the series. James and the Cavaliers made the playoffs again in 2007, where they were swept by the San Antonio Spurs.

He is already being measured against the greatest players of all time. During only his second season, one national sports magazine featured him on the front cover with the headline: "Best ever?"

Only time will tell how the player nicknamed "King James" will measure up. But based on his start in the NBA, the sky could very well be the limit.

"I don't call him 'King James,'" said Minnesota Timberwolves star Kevin Garnett. "I call him 'The Gift.' A gift for Cleveland and the league."[6]

James goes up for a dunk on a breakaway.

CAREER STATISTICS

YEAR	TEAM	G	MIN	FGM-A	FG%	FTM-A
03–04	Cleveland	79	3,122	622–1,492	0.417	347–46(
04–05	Cleveland	80	3,388	795–1,684	0.472	477–63(
05–06	Cleveland	79	3,361	875–1,823	0.480	601–814
06-07	Cleveland	78	3,190	772–1,621	0.476	489–70
Career		316	13,061	3,064–6,620	0.463	1,914–2,61

NOTE: He was disqualified from one game in 2004–05 season.

KEY:
G = Games Played
MIN = Minutes Played
FGM-A = Field Goals Made-Attempted
FG% = Field Goal Percentage
FTM-A = Free Throws Made-Attempted
FT% = Free Throw Percentage
REB = Rebounds
AST = Assists
STL = Steals
BLK = Blocked Shots
PTS = Points Scored
AVG = Points Per Game Average

FT%	REB	AST	STL	BLK	PTS	AVG
0.754	432	465	130	58	1,654	20.9
0.750	588	577	177	52	2,175	27.2
0.738	556	521	123	66	2,478	31.4
0.698	526	470	125	55	2,132	27.3
0.733	2,102	2,033	555	231	8,439	26.7

CAREER ACHIEVEMENTS

★ Named NBA Rookie of the Year in 2003-04 becoming first Cavalier and youngest player ever to receive the award.

★ One of three rookies in NBA history to average at least 20 points, 5 rebounds, and 5 assists in one season (Oscar Robertson, Michael Jordan).

★ Named NBA Eastern Conference Rookie of the Month every month of the season (November–April), becoming first Cavalier to accomplish that feat.

★ Became youngest player to score 1,000 points in NBA history and the youngest to score 40 points in a game.

★ Scored most points in an NBA debut by any prep-to-pro player with 25 points on October 29, 2003, at Sacramento.

★ Became youngest player to ever score 5,000 points at 21 years, 22 days when he scored 51 points on January 21, 2006.

HIGH SCHOOL CAREER ACHIEVEMENTS
(ST. VINCENT-ST. MARY, AKRON, OHIO):

★ Named consensus 2003 National High School Player of the Year.

★ Named *Parade* High School Boys Basketball Player of the Year as a junior and senior, becoming first repeat winner in the 47-year history of the award.

★ Named *USA Today* and Gatorade Player of the Year as both a junior and senior.

★ Led St. Vincent-St. Mary to three state championships in four seasons.

★ Named Mr. Basketball for the state of Ohio by the Associated Press for three straight seasons beginning with his sophomore year.

★ Named to *USA Today* All-USA First Team for three consecutive seasons beginning as a sophomore.

★ Named the MVP of McDonald's All American High School Basketball Game, the EA Sports Roundball Classic, and the Jordan Capital Classic.

★ Became the first sophomore ever chosen for *USA Today* All-USA First Team.

CHAPTER NOTES

CHAPTER 1. OPENING NIGHT

1. Ian Whittell, "James Lays Early Claim to Jordan's Crown," *The Times* (United Kingdom), October 31, 2003, p. 52.

2. Mark Heisler, "Debut Should be LeBronzed," *Los Angeles Times*, October 30, 2003, Part D, p. 1.

3. Rachel Nichols, "Cavs' James Shines in NBA Debut," *Washington Post*, October 30, 2003, Sports, D01.

4. Mark Heisler, "Debut Should be LeBronzed," *Los Angeles Times*, October 30, 2003, Part D, p. 1.

5. Rachel Nichols, "Cavs' James Shines in NBA Debut," *Washington Post*, October 30, 2003, Sports, D01.

6. Roscoe Nance, "On the Court of Kings, James Has a Regal Start," *USA Today*, October 31, 2003. Sports, p. 05c.

7. Ibid.

8. Sam Smith, "James' Opening Act an Electric One," *Chicago Tribune*, October 30, 2003, Sports.

CHAPTER 2. GROWING UP IN AKRON

1. Greg Wahl, "Ahead of his Class," *Sports Illustrated*, February 18, 2002, p. 62.

2. Ibid.

3. Jack McCallum, "You Gotta Carry That Weight," *Sports Illustrated*, October 27, 2003, p. 68.

4. "King James Holds Court," *Sports Illustrated for Kids*, February 2005, p. 18.

5. Ibid.

6. Terry Pluto, "LeBron James, Once a Lanky Kid, Has Come a Long Way to the NBA," *Akron Beacon Journal*, April 20, 2004.

7. Ibid.

8. Greg Wahl, "Ahead of his Class," *Sports Illustrated*, February 18, 2002, p. 62.

9. "King James Holds Court," *Sports Illustrated for Kids*, February 2005, p. 18.

10. Terry Pluto, "LeBron James, Once a Lanky Kid, Has Come a Long Way in the NBA," *Akron Beacon Journal*, April 20, 2004.

CHAPTER 3. THE "FAB FOUR" AND THEN SOME MORE

1. Michael Holley, "Akron Prep Star a Jump Ahead of the Pack," *Chicago Tribune,* November 23, 2001.

2. Gregg Doyel, "Ohio High School Star Considers Entering Draft Following High School Junior Year," *Charlotte* (NC) *Observer*, July 11, 2001.

3. Seth Davis, "Boys of Summer," *Sports Illustrated*, July 23, 2001.

4. Ibid.

5. Ibid.

CHAPTER 4. THAT CHAMPIONSHIP SEASON

1. Dick Jeradi, "Ohio Prep Player Gets National Stage Thursday Night," *Philadelphia Daily News*, December 11, 2002.

2. David Lee Morgan, Jr., "LeBron James Says He Hasn't Ruled Out College," *Akron Beacon Journal*, October 17, 2002.

3. "King James Holds Court," *Sports Illustrated for Kids*, February 2005, p. 18.

4. David Lee Morgan, Jr., "LeBron James Records a Low-Key Triple-Double," *Akron Beacon Journal*, December 7, 2002.

5. David DuPree, "High School Phenom Shows He Has All The Tools," *USA Today*, December 13, 2002.

6. Ibid.

7. Stephanie Storm, "LeBron James Makes His Team Better in Win Over Top-Ranked Oak Hill," *Akron Beacon Journal*, December 12, 2002.

8. Ibid.

9. Brian Windhorst, "James, Ohio Team Look to Vault to. No. 1 Ranking," *Akron Beacon Journal*, January 5, 2003.

10. Ray Glier, "James-led Ohio Team Takes No. 1," *USA Today*, January 7, 2003, Sports, p. 10c.

11. Sam Mellinger, "Hoops Phenom no Stranger to Special Treatment," *Kansas City Star*, January 20, 2003.

12. "Hoops Star Cleared in Hummer Probe," CBS News, January 27, 2003.

13. "LeBron Nets 52 in Hoop Return," *Toronto Star*, February 9, 2003, Sports, p. E05.

14. Brian Windhorst, "LeBron James Ends High School Career With Another State Crown," *Akron Beacon Journal*, March 22, 2003.

15. Jon Siegel, "James Stages Classic Show for MCI Fans," *The Washington Times*, April 18, 2003.

CHAPTER 5. ROOKIE SEASON

1. Tom Reed, "Signing for Millions Doesn't Deter LeBron From Attending Class, School Cafeteria," *Akron Beacon Journal*, May 24, 2003.

2. David DuPree, "King James Enjoys Coronation," *USA Today*, June 27, 2003, Sports, p. 01c.

3. Stephen F. Holder, "LeBron James Brings Out Showtime in Summer League," Knight-Ridder/Tribune News Service, July 8, 2003.

4. Bob Finnan, "Early to Rise," *Sporting News*, October 20, 2003.

5. "Wonderkind LeBron Shows That He Belongs," *Toronto Star*, November 1, 2003.

6. Ibid.

7. Roscoe Nance, "James King of Road During First Week in NBA," *USA Today*, November 5, 2003, Sports. p. 03c.

8. Brian Windhorst, "Cavs Score Rare Victory Over Sixers," *Akron Beacon Journal*, November 15, 2003.

9. Brian Windhorst, "James Takes Benching in Stride," *Akron Beacon Journal*, December 4, 2003.

10. Ibid.

11. Sam Smith, "LeBron James Not an MJ Clone, But He Can be Something Special," *Chicago Tribune*, December 21, 2003.

12. K.C. Johnson. "With Jordan Watching, LeBron Puts on a Show in Chicago," *Chicago Tribune*, December 21, 2003.

13. Don Daly, "LeBron, Carmelo Compete for Feats," *Washington Times*, April 1, 2004, Sports, p. C01.

14. Tom Reed, "LeBron Waiting, Watching, Wondering During Offseason," *Akron Beacon Journal*, April 15, 2004.

15. Terry Pluto, "LeBron Exceeds All Expectations," *Akron Beacon Journal*, April 15, 2004.

CHAPTER 6. JAMES' JOURNEY

1. Adrian Wojnarowski, "Likeable LeBron has been Groomed for Stardom," *The Record* (Bergen County, N.J.), November 10, 2003.

2. Roscoe Nance, "LeBron Just Plays it Cool," *USA Today*, June 24, 2003, Sports, p. 01c.

3. Mark Emmons, "James Masters the Burdens of Hype," *San Jose Mercury News*, January 16, 2004.

4. Brian Windhorst, "James Looks Back on NBA Experience," *Akron Beacon Journal*, February 7, 2004.

5. Adrian Wojnarowski, "Likeable LeBron Has Been Groomed for Stardom," *The Record* (Bergen County, N.J.), November 10, 2003.

6. Charles P. Pierce, "The Future is Now," *Sports Illustrated*, February 21, 2005, p. 64.

7. Sean Gregory, "King James," *Time*, January 31, 2005, p. 58.

8. "King James Holds Court," *Sports Illustrated for Kids*, February 2005, p. 18.

9. David Lee Morgan, Jr., "James Backs PE Program for Schoolchildren," *Akron Beacon Journal*, September 7, 2003.

10. Theresa Howard, "$16 million and counting ... LeBron Racks up Scores of Ad Deals," *USA Today*, August 18, 2004, Money, p. 03b.

11. "LeBron Happy, But Won't Give Baby Details," *The Associated Press*, October 8, 2004.

CHAPTER 7. GOING FOR 50

1. David Feschuk, "King James Rules!," *Toronto Star*, March 21, 2005, Sports, p. D01.

2. Mary Schmitt Boyer, "Fabulous, Futile 56 James Breaks Two Records, but Cavs Fall on Road Again," *Cleveland Plain Dealer*, March 21, 2005, p. C1.

3. David Feschuk, "King James Rules!," *Toronto Star*, March 21, 2005, Sports, p. D01.

4. Ibid.

5. The Associated Press, "LeBron's 56 Not Enough as Cavs Fall to Raptors," *The Grand Rapids Press*, March 21, 2005, p. C3.

6. Ibid.

CHAPTER 8. THE BEAT GOES ON

1. "Rockets Punish Cavs," *Toronto Star*, December 30, 2004, Sports, p. C09.

2. "Notebook," *Toronto Star*, January 3, 2005, Sports, p. C06.

3. Ibid.

4. Ibid.

5. "Last Night in the NBA," *Toronto Star*, January 4, 2005, Sports, p. D06.

6. Charles P. Pierce, "The Future is Now," *Sports Illustrated*, February 21, 2005, p. 64.

7. David Dupree, "James Makes Olympic Impressions," *USA Today*, July 28, 2004, Sports, p. 02c.

8. Dave Feschuk, "LeBron's Act Just Got Better," *Toronto Star*, October 30, 2004, Sports, p. E02.

9. David Dupree, "Cavaliers' James Leads Young Stars in MVP Hunt," *USA Today*, November 30, 2004, Sports, p. 07c.

10. David Dupree, "Lessons Learned in Athens," *USA Today*, January 4, 2005, Sports, p. 13c.

CHAPTER 9. A GIFT FOR CLEVELAND AND THE LEAGUE

1. Rob Gillies, "LeBron's Big Game Not Enough to Put Cavs in Playoffs," *Associated Press Sports*, April 20, 2005.

2. "LeBron Sets Scoring Mark," *Newark Star Ledger*, November 14, 2005, Sports p. 040.

3. Cleveland Cavaliers Web site, http://www.nba.com/Cavaliers/, August 29, 2005.

4. Tom Reed, "LeBron and Friends Take the Akron Bike Route for a Good Cause," *Akron Beacon Journal*, June 24, 2005.

5. Ibid.

6. "LeBron Faces the Big 2-0," *Toronto Star*, December 29, 2004, Sports, p. D09.

GLOSSARY

assist—The last pass to a teammate that leads directly to a field goal; the scorer must move immediately toward the basket for the passer to be credited with an assist; only one assist can be credited per field goal

blocked shot—The successful deflection of a shot by touching part of the ball on its way to the basket, thereby preventing a field goal.

draft—The method by which NBA teams annually select college or foreign players to their teams. It is designed to promote balanced competition in the NBA.

dunk—When a player close to the basket jumps and strongly throws the ball down into it; an athletic, creative shot used to intimidate opponents.

floor—The area of the court within the end lines and sidelines.

forwards—The two players on the court for a team who are usually smaller than the center and bigger than the guards; often a team's highest scorers.

foul—An action by a player that breaks the rules but is not a floor violation, such as traveling with the basketball; a player who fouls another player is penalized by a change in possession or free-throw opportunities for the other team.

foul line—The line 15 feet from the backboard and parallel to the end line from which players shoot free throws.

guards—The two players on each team who are the smallest on the court; they usually handle setting up plays and passing to teammates closer to the basket.

layup—A shot taken after driving to the basket by leaping up under the basket and using one hand to bank the ball off the backboard into it.

MVP (Most Valuable Player)—An award recognizing the NBA player who contributed most to the regular season or to the Finals.

NBA (National Basketball Association)—A professional league created in 1949 that now has 30 teams in the United States and Canada.

out of bounds—The area outside of and including the end lines and sidelines.

pass—When a passer throws the ball to a teammate; used to start plays, move the ball downcourt, keep it away from defenders, and get it to a shooter.

period—Any quarter, half, or overtime segment of a game.

rebound—When a player grabs a ball that is coming off the rim or backboard after a shot attempt.

rookie—A player in his first NBA season.

roster—The list of players on a team.

three-pointer—A field goal worth three points because the shooter had both feet on the floor behind the three-point line when he released the ball; also counts if one foot is behind the line while the other is in the air.

tip-off—The initial jump ball that starts the game.

triple-double—When a player scores double-digits in three categories during one game (points, assists, and rebounds are most common, but it can also be blocks or steals).

FOR MORE INFORMATION

FURTHER READING

Carr, Austin. *Tales from the Cleveland Cavaliers: The Rookie Season of LeBron James.* Champaign, Ill.: Sports Publishing, 2004.

Jones, Ryan. *King James: Believe the Hype, the LeBron James Story.* New York: St. Martin's Press, 2003.

Morgan Jr., David Lee. *LeBron James, Rise of a Star.* Cleveland: Gray & Company, 2003.

Robinson, B.J. *LeBron James, King of the Court.* East Cleveland: Forest Hill Publishing, 2005.

WEB LINKS

James' profile on NBA.com
http://www.nba.com/playerfile/lebron_james/

The official LeBron James Web site
http://www.lebronjames.com

James' player page on ESPN.com
http://sports.espn.go.com/nba/players/profile?statsId=3704

James' player page on SI.com
http://sportsillustrated.cnn.com/basketball/nba/players/3704/

The official Web site of the Cleveland Cavaliers
http://www.nba.com/cavaliers/

The official Web site of the NBA
http://www.nba.com

INDEX